My Little Red Wagon

July 19, 2010

Dear Lexy —

Welcome to the Radio Flyer Team! We are counting on you to help us keep on bringing smiles and creating warm memories that last a lifetime!

Sincerely,

Robert Pasin

♡ ☺ 🛒

My Little Red Wagon

Radio Flyer Memories

Robert Pasin and Paul Pasin

**Andrews McMeel
Publishing**

Kansas City

www.andrewsmcmeel.com

99 00 01 02 03 TWP 10 9 8 7 6 5 4 3 2 1

Library of Congress Cataloging-in-Publication Data
My little red wagon : Radio flyer memories / [edited by] Robert Pasin and Paul Pasin.
    p.   cm.
    ISBN 0-7407-0044-8 (pbk.)
  1. Radio Flyer Inc. 2. Wagons Anecdotes. 3. Toys—United States Anecdotes I. Pasin, Robert.
II. Radio Flyer Inc.
TS2301.T7M9 1999
688.6—dc21   99-31516
                                               CIP

Design by Holly Camerlinck

www.radioflyer.com

ATTENTION: SCHOOLS AND BUSINESSES

❖

To Antonio Pasin,
the dreamer
who made dreams come true
for millions of boys and girls

❖

❖ CONTENTS ❖

❖ PREFACE ❖

Everybody has a Radio Flyer story. As grandsons of Radio Flyer's founder, whenever we meet people and tell them about our family business, people tell us about "the little red wagon I had as a kid." Every story is unique and every time we hear these stories, we are warmly reminded of how this little red wagon, the product of an immigrant boy's dream, has created so many other dreams by nurturing children's imaginations.

When we read the thousands of incredible stories and saw the photos that poured into our offices in celebration of Radio Flyer's eightieth anniversary, we were quite simply overwhelmed. From the boy in Indiana who lost his wagon in a tragic train accident, only to receive his replacement Radio Flyer over sixty years later, to the girl in New York in the 1950s, whose wagon taught her that she (like the boys) could race and dream, we were moved to tears by the powerful emotions chronicled in each entry.

Antonio Pasin's story is the classic immigrant success story. A man who was little more than a boy when he came to America, Antonio dreamed of making a wagon that was affordable to "Every Boy, Every Girl." Antonio succeeded and in the process created a vehicle for millions of kids' imaginations. We know that our grandfather would take enormous pride in this book and in what Radio Flyer means to America. We are proud that our family continues to pull this little red wagon and we look forward to another eighty years of creating wagons that nurture the wonder of childhood.

❖ Robert Pasin and Paul Pasin

My Little Red Wagon

History of a Cultural Icon

The year was 1914. Like millions of immigrants, Antonio Pasin was welcomed to the land of opportunity by the Statue of Liberty. With his head full of dreams, and his feet firmly planted on the ground, sixteen-year-old Antonio stepped off the boat from Italy.

He hardly had a cent in his pocket—but he did have smarts, energy, and a dream. Antonio was an Old World craftsman whose family had designed and built furniture and cabinets for generations in Italy. His desire to come to America and pursue his dream was so strong that his family sold their mule to pay for his ticket.

Antonio started by building phonograph cabinets in his one-room workshop. Soon after, he began crafting his first wooden wagons by hand. He made wagons at night and peddled them during the day, carrying around small samples in a battered suitcase. Business grew steadily, and in 1923 he hired a helper and founded the Liberty Coaster Wagon Company, which he named after the Statue of Liberty.

Antonio saw how his wagons made dreams come true for kids across America, but he also knew that traditional handcrafting could produce relatively few wagons each day. He turned to the auto industry for inspiration, and began to use metal-stamping technology to produce his wagons. With his eye for innovation, Pasin applied mass-production techniques to wagon making, creating the first mass-market wagon that was, as its tagline said, "For every boy. For every girl." This earned him the nickname "Little Ford."

By 1930, his company operated under a new name—Radio Steel & Manufacturing Company—and was already the world's largest producer of coaster wagons. However, these were hard times for America, and during this period Americans learned how to make do, or simply do without. But even in tough times they dreamed of a better life for their children and continued to demand the basic value that Radio Flyer delivered. Antonio often said with pride that not once during the Depression did his factory produce less than 1,500 wagons a day.

The names Pasin gave his toy wagons were intended to capture the spirit of the times. For the wagon that has become an icon, the popular Model 18, he chose the word *Radio*, because everyone was fascinated by radio, the new wireless invention of fellow Italian Guglielmo Marconi, and *Flyer*, which gave a nod to the wonder of flight.

In the late 1980s, the company took the name of its most popular product, Radio Flyer. It continues to produce wagons, wheelbarrows, and specialty products in the same factory built by its founder.

Antonio Pasin shared his Radio Flyer dream with everyone he knew. Today, Antonio's grandsons own and manage Radio Flyer, inspired by their grandfather's dream and the challenge of upholding the Radio Flyer traditions of innovation, quality, and value for generations to come.

In celebration of its eightieth anniversary, the Radio Flyer company sponsored a contest called "Radio Flyer Memories," which invited people to share stories, anecdotes, and photos of their own Radio Flyer wagons. The results are collected in this nostalgic and heartwarming look at the history of the "little red wagon" and its unique place in twentieth-century history.

Radio Flyer Timeline

1914   Antonio Pasin arrives in the United States from Italy.

1917   Pasin begins producing toy coaster wagons in his one-room shop.

1923   Pasin hires assistants and creates the Liberty Coaster Wagon Company.

1927   Liberty Coaster begins making stamped metal wagons called Radio Flyers.

1930   The company is renamed Radio Steel & Manufacturing and is already the world's largest producer of toy coaster wagons.

1933   Radio Steel's forty-five-foot-tall Coaster Boy is one of the most popular exhibits at the Chicago's World's Fair. It offers miniature wagons for twenty-five cents.

1934   The Streak-O-Lite, modeled after the popular streamlined Zephyr train, is the company's first specialty wagon. It features working headlights and controls.

1941   The company goes to war, turning out steel "blitz cans" for military vehicles.

1957   In response to the baby boomer generation, the company introduces a line of garden carts to make lawn care easier in the fast-growing suburbs.

1977   The company pioneers new wagon safety features, including a patented "no-pinch" ball joint and a controlled turning radius to prevent tipping over.

1987   The company is renamed Radio Flyer Inc., after its most popular product.

1994   Radio Flyer introduces its first all-plastic wagon, the Trailblazer.

1996   Leadership of Radio Flyer Inc. is passed to Antonio's grandsons, the third generation.

1997   Radio Flyer celebrates its eightieth anniversary by constructing the World's Largest Wagon™, a twenty-six-foot tall salute to America's original little red wagon.

Fifty Years of Radio Flyin'

BILL AND BARBARA ANDERSON
ROSWELL, GEORGIA

The photo of Bill and Margaret has always been a family favorite. When we opened the grandchildren's Radio Flyer wagon Christmas morning and we saw the contest we knew we had to enter. Grandpa Bill was visiting the grandchildren, who live in Holland, which made the pictures with them possible. Long-distance phone calls to little sis Margaret helped with the script for the photos. We had a wonderful time putting this together.

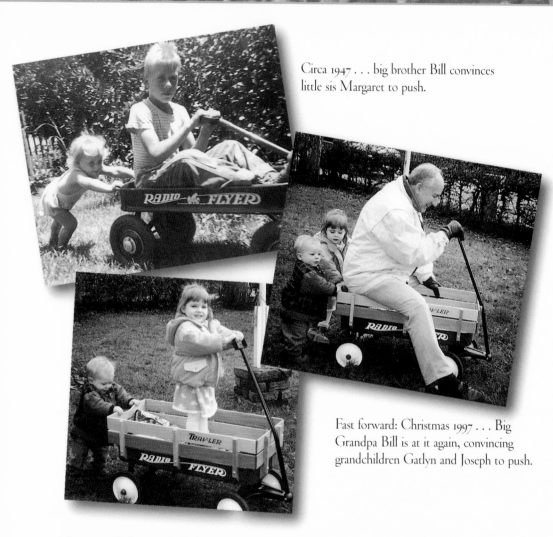

Circa 1947 . . . big brother Bill convinces little sis Margaret to push.

Fast forward: Christmas 1997 . . . Big Grandpa Bill is at it again, convincing grandchildren Gatlyn and Joseph to push.

Big sister Gatlyn gets little brother Joseph to continue the family tradition.

❖ FIRST PLACE ❖

KAREN M. FUNK
SANTA CRUZ, CALIFORNIA

In the 1940s' Highland Park area of Los Angeles, extended families crowded into gracious old homes to save money and space during the war. Playmates abounded, and we all had clip-on skates—but my family owned a bright red Radio Flyer! The only family with more prestige among the kids was the one with the TV. That Flyer got a good workout every day coasting a load of kids down the Meridian Street hill to steep Avenue Fifty-seven at breakneck speed, just making the left-turn corner and nearly flying for real halfway down Avenue Fifty-seven to our "bail-out" lawn.

That's me—the redhead in front by the handle. My best friend Judy French is behind me, my sister Marilyn and baby cousin Theresa behind her. My brother Dennis is the hatless "cowboy" in left rear, the neighborhood brat, Marty Price, at right rear, and my first love, John Mosteller, is on his bike behind Dennis.

Second Place
Winners

❖ SECOND PLACE ❖

TIM SCHEY
SANTA MONICA, CALIFORNIA

When I was four my father took me for a walk every morning. One night I noticed a bright red wagon inside the garage of our neighbors, an elderly couple I'd never once seen smile. Tugging my dad's sleeve, I asked if we could borrow it, but he said no, that it didn't belong to us. Each evening after that I begged again. "I'm sorry," he would say.

When Dad asked what I wanted for my fifth birthday, I told him I only wanted to take walks together. That night the old man was outside, and for once I didn't ask about the wagon. Suddenly Dad stopped, led me back to the man's yard. He introduced himself and explained about the wagon and my request.

The man's stern look melted. His eyes grew moist. He told me that the wagon had belonged to their only child, Hardy, and that leukemia had taken the boy when he was seven.

Old Mr. Griffith looked down at me, smiling through his pain. He said he wanted me to use the wagon because his son no longer could, and

right there he gave me Hardy's Radio Flyer.

From then on the wagon became part of our nightly walks. More importantly, I adopted a "granddfather" whom I grew to love. I now use Hardy's classic Radio Flyer—still in fine working order—to pull my own son, Dakota. Much more than a child-hood toy, to me it represents the priceless bond between father and son—and the importance of enjoying this gift while we can.

The Vehicle to Freedom

MAGGI HALL
SAINT AUGUSTINE, FLORIDA

To a child of the 1940s, a special toy and sharp imagination brought untold adventures. I know, I was that child; my special toy was given to me on my third Christmas, a shiny red Radio Flyer with black rubber tires, metal hubcaps, and a bed deep enough to carry serious material and an even more serious little girl.

That wagon became my vehicle to Mars, my horse that led to the desolation of cattle-rustling thieves, even the fire truck that saved our neighborhood. I'd sit with my right leg bent under, nestled in the wagon, my left leg dangling over the side, foot pushing hard against the pavement, propelling me forward toward five . . . seven . . . ten . . .

My Radio Flyer lasted into the 1970s, when my three-year-old was given the privilege of riding in that old chariot attached behind her grandfather's lawn mower. Watching from the front porch of our homestead, I finally realized what my wise parents had always known: The joys and freedoms of childhood are intrinsically connected to the ownership of a Radio Flyer.

❖ Second Place ❖

Brigid Anne Winn
Longmont, Colorado

❖ Second Place ❖

Rachel Alcock
Baton Rouge, Louisiana

❖ Second Place ❖

STEPHANIE BISHOP
KINGSPORT, TENNESSEE

Joshua and Jamie love being pulled in their Radio Flyer. Together or alone, uphill or down, over bumps and rocky roads, they share many memories in their little red wagon. Thanks, Radio Flyer, for helping make so many special memories!

❖ SECOND PLACE ❖

ANDREW ROBB, JR.
CHICAGO, ILLINOIS

In 1929 my Pa gave me a Radio Flyer wagon! It was my most prized possession. I could ride it as fast as the wind. I used the wagon to carry groceries, bakery goods, lumber, and firewood for the kitchen stove.

One day while going for firewood I was struck by a train. The wagon, my left arm, and shoulder were horribly demolished.

I always wanted that Radio Flyer coaster wagon. In 1995, when I was seventy-five years old, my dream came true. My wife presented me with a most beautiful replacement!

My Radio Flyer

THOMAS J. ITRICH
BLOOMINGDALE, ILLINOIS

The year was 1946 in Chicago—the Western frontier—where my Radio Flyer became my stagecoach. It was my main means of transportation. I can still remember sitting on one leg while pushing off with the other. At four years old I could get up a pretty good speed until I went careening off the sidewalk into a rut. This caused me to come to an abrupt stop, at which point I would quickly yank the wagon back on course and ride like the wind! I left my Radio Flyer outside for quick get-aways, like the cowboy left his horse tied to a post. With your wagon and my imagination, anything was possible!

❖ SECOND PLACE ❖

BARBARA DAWN MEYER
MORTON GROVE, ILLINOIS

This photo was taken September 19, 1950. This was the beginning of my Radio Flyer red wagon use. My father made several sacrifices to see that I had a wagon for my birthday, which I did not know at the time. We lived in a small rural town in Wisconsin, and money was scarce, to say the least. I loved my Radio Flyer wagon and used it for hauling teddy bears, baby chicks, kittens, and puppies. Later, I used it to haul hay bales to feed thirty head of cattle. I hauled four bales with the help of either my mom, sister, or brother—which had to be done twice daily. I left home in 1965, and lost track of my Radio Flyer wagon. It was handed down to my younger sister and brother, who used it for odd jobs on our farm. I will always cherish my memories of its use.

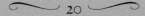

❖ Second Place ❖

Mrs. Arthur Rossi
Shrewsbury, Massachusetts

Finally—a tribute to our red Radio Flyer! It brings back many pleasant memories, my favorite being able to pull my first two grandchildren around our circle drive. The Radio Flyer saved us from buying an expensive multiple stroller.

Now, twenty-four years and eleven more grandchildren later, we've never been without our red wagon. It was everything to each child—a covered wagon, a trailer-truck, a hauler, and even a work vehicle!

Since the birth of my first child in 1951, there has always been a Radio Flyer in our garage ready for fun and, hopefully, my great-grandchildren!

❖ SECOND PLACE ❖

RONNI LEA FOX
BUFFALO, NEW YORK

My Radio Flyer was my liberator. In 1955, a girl was taught what she couldn't be or do. My Radio Flyer said, "Can too!" It taught me to work hard for what I wanted. You can't soar down a hill if you don't trudge up it first! Wrecks taught me to deal with adversity, make repairs, and move on. After I insisted the boys let me compete in their races, Dad starting calling it my "suffragette wagon." It taught me I could compete successfully—and equally—with anyone. Thanks, Radio Flyer!

❖ SECOND PLACE ❖

SCOTT HALEY
RALEIGH, NORTH CAROLINA

My one-year-old daughter, Megan, received a Town and Country wagon for Christmas in 1997. I read the Radio Flyer booklet as I assembled the wagon. I had received a Radio Rancher for Christmas as a youngster, and upon seeing a picture of the wagon, I remembered all of the fun I had as a child in my own Rancher.

Megan loved her new wagon. So many memories flooded my mind and tears swelled in my eyes as I saw the joy in her little face. Radio Flyer is neither mere legend nor small tradition. It has become a way of life for many generations and continues to create lifetime memories for young and old kids. Thanks a million for the memories!

❖ Second Place ❖

S. Davis Stone
Rapid City, South Dakota

What a memory the Radio Flyer brings to mind! Our two little boys, Bill, two years, and John, eight months, had a dad who was in the Navy in World War II. We lived in a little cabin and it mattered little that we had no car, as gasoline was severely rationed.

About a quarter of a mile down the road were Indian tents and few houses. This was Saint Patrick Street in Rapid City, South Dakota, in 1945. Since I walked wherever I went, I wanted a wagon, as carrying a child in each arm balanced on my hip was too difficult. But it was wartime and there was no metal to make new Radio Flyers. So I walked the residential area of Rapid City looking into people's yards. If they had a wagon, I stopped and asked if they had children to use the wagon. After many days of fruitless searching I found a red Radio Flyer! The children who had used it were grown, so the lady sold it to me for five dollars. It was a little rusty, but otherwise in dandy shape. What a help that wagon was! And the boys loved to go with me after the mail to see if there was a letter from Dad. It was about a quarter mile to the mailbox and one and a half miles to downtown. I was twenty-one years old and full of energy, so we had many happy trips. Bill would pat the side of our Radio Flyer and say, "Get up, Horsey!" wanting me to run, and John would burst into giggles as I walked faster. The wagon even had some room for groceries and necessities, along with the boys.

We had a total of five children who loved "taking turns" riding and pulling the red wagon. It held up well and even lasted for our first grandson.

When the Radio Flyer had to be retired, I planted it with moss roses and it graced the railing of our front porch. And strangely enough, the name Radio Flyer still showed plainly on its side. After so many years of happy use, it was practically a family member!

My eyes grow moist as nostalgia overtakes me. I am now seventy-four, with ten grandchildren and five great-grandchildren, but I thank God for the happy memories recalled by thinking about our red Radio Flyer.

❖ Second Place ❖

MICHELLE PANNELL
MISSION VIEJO, CALIFORNIA

Our "little red wagon" memory is one that is actually about our son, who is two years old. Since my husband and I both grew up with Radio Flyers we knew that when our son turned one, we would buy him one. You can't ever be too ready for your first red wagon! Ever since then, he pulls his toys around in it, "reading" his books. When we tour the neighborhood garage sales, Cody is in his wagon. History shows it is a good durable wagon to pass on through generations.

Third Place Winners

❖ THIRD PLACE ❖

CAROLYN D. OWEN
ALBANY, OREGON

My brothers and I discovered it in Grandma's basement. A genuine Radio Flyer! It was covered with dust, but well used at one time. In a heartbeat the old wagon was reborn! A red streak zipped down the street on a San Francisco hill. We were whooping and hollering as the "Red Racer" flew with amazing speed. Dad came out to see what all the racket was about. When he saw us his features changed. He was smiling. He was remembering.

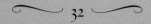

The Little Red Wagon to the Rescue

SHARON OBERNE
NORFOLK, VIRGINIA

My best memory of the little red wagon was when my younger brother and I used it one Christmas Eve. Our family was poor and we wanted a Christmas tree. At a local gas station, the owner was giving away trees that weren't sold. My brother and I weren't strong enough to carry one home. So, we used the wagon. We took turns slowly pulling the wagon down a bumpy road that led home, and later, we sat in the wagon waiting for Santa.

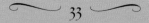

❖ THIRD PLACE ❖

JANET LOCKWOOD
CINCINNATI, OHIO

You are looking at a toddler who was very interested in the solid construction of his little red wagon. This laid the foundation for David's ability to rebuild the engine of another classic vehicle at the age of seventeen—his 1955 Chevy.

David's little red wagon set the stage for his inquiring mind to look at the overall picture and figure out the different parts of the total project, and we thought he was just having a great time! David went on to graduate from college and become a high school physics and chemistry teacher. Did his little red wagon help him on this important path? We like to think so.

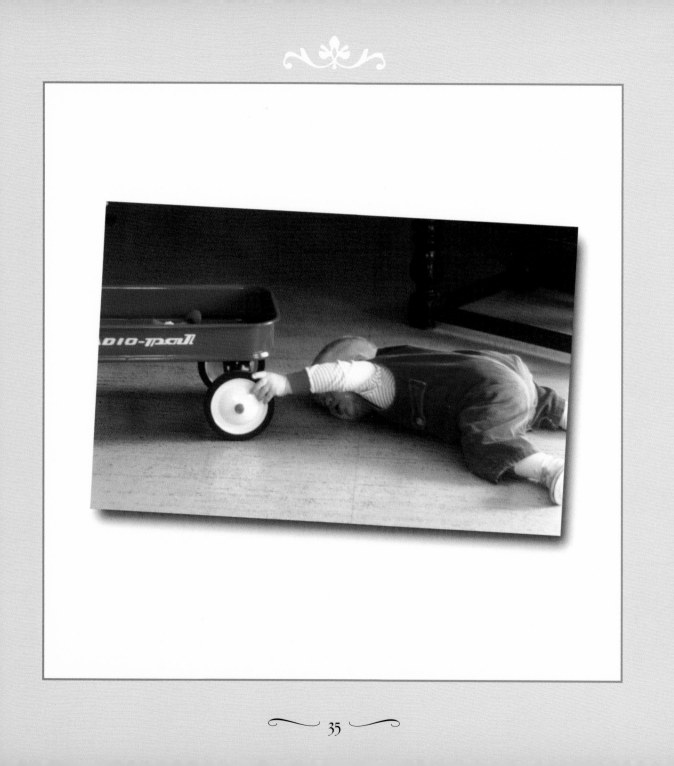

✦ Third Place ✦

Alice Warner Lewis
New Era, Michigan

Flying down the city sidewalk in his Liberty Coaster wagon was the delight of my five-year-old brother in the spring of 1923.

Born in December 1917, while his father was away in World War I, he didn't live to celebrate his and Radio Flyer's eightieth birthdays. He would be pleased to know that his first great-grandnephews are already riding around the farm in New Era, Michigan, in their new, shiny-red Model 89 Radio Flyer Wagon.

❖ Third Place ❖

Laurie Hilyer
Salt Lake City, Utah

Carlie, her dog Bo, and their Radio Flyer have been constant companions for years. The wagon has hauled wildflowers, rocks, sticks, snow, dolls, and even Bo himself. Carlie is now four and the Radio Flyer is still rolling behind her.

This summer day, Carlie, almost two, crawled into the wagon for a nap while Bo stood guard.

❖ THIRD PLACE ❖

DORIS BRADSHAW
VALLEY MILLS, TEXAS

The Christmas of 1945 I was ten and my brother was one. He was getting a Radio Flyer for Christmas, but on Christmas Eve our cousin decided to be born. My uncle was sick with the flu, so our father and mother took my aunt to the hospital. They returned home about eleven that night. My little brother awoke and helped Santa (Father) finish assembling his Radio Flyer. Of course, he was too young to know the difference—he was just glad Santa had brought him his wagon on Christmas morning!

❖ THIRD PLACE ❖

BOB ZECHMAN
PLANO, TEXAS

Back in 1967, when we bought our Radio Flyer Wagon, we took it everywhere—walks, parks, zoos, flea markets! One day one of our children was being pulled along when a car suddenly backed out of a drive. The car hit our wagon but only bent one side. The wagon is built so indestructibly that our child was saved from any serious harm. If it wasn't for the wagon, one of our six children might not be here today. We still have that wagon and will always have fond memories of it.

❖ Third Place ❖

Howard W. Brown
Raleigh, North Carolina

I dreaded walking up those attic stairs, dust hiding memories—stored like past winter storms. I glanced around the collections: steamer trunks, furniture, and clothes whose wearers danced to vinyl records. Picking through like the auctioneer coming, I accidentally stumbled on something red: my Radio Flyer. Sitting down, I ran my hands across the cold smooth metal—hearing the laughter as Dad pulled us across the yard.

My wife called, "Did you find something?" I silently nodded as I headed out with wagon in tow—holding it from the auctioneer's call.

❖ THIRD PLACE ❖

LORETTA HENRY
FORT WAYNE, INDIANA

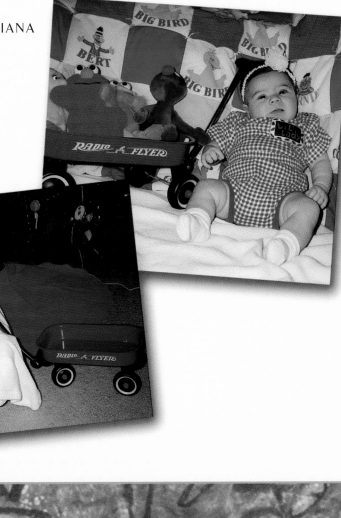

❖ Third Place ❖

GAYLE R. M. HALL
MUNDELEIN, ILLINOIS

Nineteen years ago, we as a family adopted our now twenty-six-year-old daughter. She is severely handicapped with cerebral palsy. Though the entire family has always helped in the care of our Missy, my son Blake, now twenty-nine, became Missy's true buddy. I will always remember how he would load her in our Radio Flyer wagon and take her around the block so she could sit for hours and watch him play ball with his friends. The Radio Flyer wagon gave her a window to the world, and a place by her brother's side.

❖ THIRD PLACE ❖

THERESA CLISH
WARREN, MICHIGAN

It was seventeen years ago when my beautiful niece Jennifer was born with the medical condition club foot. She would need several operations.

After the first operation Jennifer was in a lot of pain, and she cried constantly—until my sister saw a red Radio Flyer in the pediatric ward. In went a pillow, blanket, and my niece. The crying stopped instantly. For days, up and down the halls, we all took turns walking a happy baby girl in her wagon.

Jennifer had five operations. Your wagon saved our sanity, and brought happiness to a little girl.

❖ THIRD PLACE ❖

SUSAN F. JUOZITIS
TOPEKA, KANSAS

Our Radio Flyer memory lives on! Our roving garden continues to delight us with splashes of annual blooms and its handsome harvest of fall vegetables. Our true memory lies in cherishing the miracle of life through the simplicity of a child's garden.

Over ten years old, and in its "close to home" phase, Radio Flyer was retired from its post as "Soccer Saturday Caddy" and headed for the greener pastures of garden life. Its wheels encourage strategic positioning throughout the season, and grant the mobility to parade off-site to neighboring yards to share the harvest with pride and delight!

❖ THIRD PLACE ❖

FRANK AND LISA MCCOY
CEDAR RAPIDS, IOWA

This is Hayley's first pumpkin-patch visit and we took along her Radio Flyer (a gift from her grandparents, Stan and Mabel Reynolds of El Dorado, Kansas). She had a great time sampling the pumpkins!

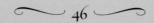

❖ THIRD PLACE ❖

ANGIE RAE TAZELAAR
SAFETY HARBOR, FLORIDA

My Grandpa Ray and I were very close. He got me my first red Radio Flyer wagon when I was eighteen months old. He used to pull me down the street and back and I laughed and laughed—it was so much fun to be with my grandpa. And still, to this day, I have that special wagon.

❖ Third Place ❖

Laleh Ramezani
Rancho Palos Verdes, California

When I was a child, my dad used to take me on my Radio Flyer to visit neighbors. He'd put a pillow in the wagon and drag me down the street. I remember those days fondly.

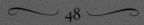

❖ THIRD PLACE ❖

BRYAN AND KATIE OGLE
POST FALLS, IDAHO

Here is our Fourth of July baby,
Brock. We hope you get as good a
laugh as we have looking at this
photo. Enjoy!

❖ THIRD PLACE ❖

SCOTT HASSELL
MOBILE, ALABAMA

I saw the article on Radio Flyers in our local paper and thought of a favorite family photo. The picture is of my grandparents. They lived on an old farm in rural Alabama. At the time this picture was taken, Grandfather was in his nineties and Grandmother in her eighties. They were still very active and living on their own on their farm. Grandfather used a wagon to haul sacks of feed. I remember coming to visit as a child and riding that wagon down the hill in front of the old farmhouse. The old wagon he used (also a Radio Flyer and in the picture) was worn out. On Christmas someone in the family gave him a new wagon. This is a picture of him taking his "girl" for a ride in his new red wagon. My Grandfather lived to one hundred and was active and living on the farm until the last few months. He used his wagon to carry anything too heavy to handle on his own. The last Christmas he was with us, my uncle gave him a miniature Radio Flyer wagon. It really made him laugh. The picture brings back fond memories of my grandparents and Radio Flyer wagons.

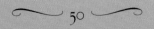

❖ THIRD PLACE ❖

EMILY H. PEAKE
RIVA, MARYLAND

Jimmy hauled everything in his Radio Flyer, but the funniest thing he carried in his wagon was an overweight English bulldog. When Jimmy picked up the handle of the wagon, Susie would jump in, ready to go for a ride. Standing on all fours, she would brace herself for a rough ride. When the ride was over—usually when Jimmy himself was worn out— she would lie down in the wagon and go to sleep.

❖ THIRD PLACE ❖

GERMAINE P. DUDLEY
WORCESTER, MASSACHUSETTS

I am seventy years old, the eldest of seven children. When I was a little girl, my parents could not afford a car, so they bought a Radio Flyer wagon. I went to the corner store and put groceries in the wagon. I pushed my brothers around; they would steer it, pretending it was a car. Dad and I went to the Farmers' Market and filled the wagon with fruits and vegetables. My brothers and sisters sat in it, and it was a carriage. Our Radio Flyer was a very important part of our family.

❖ THIRD PLACE ❖

LAURA COLLINS
DENVER, COLORADO

We grew up in the small town of Flagstaff, Arizona, and were about nine months old in the picture. The Radio Flyer wagon was as much a novelty as we were, being one of the few sets of twins in town. We were the seventh and eighth of nine children. As far as material things, we didn't have much, but we had lots of love from a mother who dedicated herself to raising us. New toys were usually for birthdays or Christmas only and shared amongst us. Larger toys were definitely a novelty around our house as they were usually too expensive, so had to be handed down from big brothers.

Twins Laura and Linda, Flagstaff, Arizona, 1949.

❖ Third Place ❖

ROBYN KING
BAY CITY, TEXAS

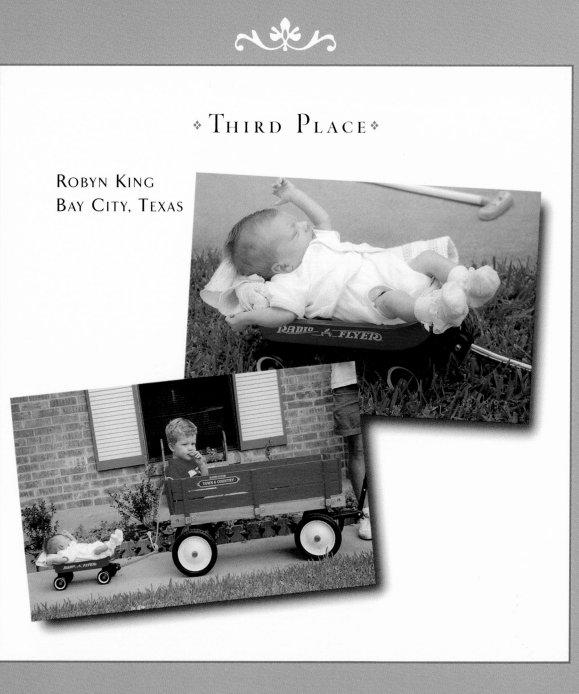

❖ Third Place ❖

Tracey Clark
Long Beach, California

❖ THIRD PLACE ❖

ALAN G. SCHMIDT
SPRINGFIELD, MISSOURI

I can think of no better testimony to the quality of Radio Flyer wagons than the two photographs I have enclosed. The top photo is of myself and was taken by my father in April 1957 as I was enjoying a backyard adventure in my wagon. The second picture, which I took, is of my son, Casey Alan, in August 1985—in the same Radio Flyer! Congratulations on your eightieth anniversary, and thanks for two generations' worth of memories and fun!

Alan Schmidt—April 1957

Casey Alan Schmidt—
August 1985

❖ Third Place ❖

ETHEL A. YOUNG
SPOKANE, WASHINGTON

❖ THIRD PLACE ❖

JULIE DUNCAN
PLANO, TEXAS

Gehrig Michael Duncan, August 1997

❖ THIRD PLACE ❖

ERIN J. KNOTEK
MOOSE PASS, ALASKA

Let's sell Kool-Aid," Paul suggested.

"Nah, my mom won't let me make it. It stains the counter," I replied.

"Don't worry—I'll make the Kool-Aid, you get the wagon!" he ordered.

Paul was six, the older man in my life (I was only five). We were two children, growing up in a town where everyone knew each other . . . where doors weren't locked and lemonade stands on a Radio Flyer could make your fortune! We lived on First Street, and in the early 1970s it was still brick. The street was very narrow, and all that passed our driveway were city trucks going to the city garage or a neighbor heading home. Yet, day in and day out, we'd sit at our perch—the Radio Flyer—and talk about all of the things we could buy with our money. (Nickels add up, you know.)

I am now thirty-one. When I think of Radio Flyers, I think of Kool-Aid stands and Paul. He sought his fame and fortune in California—sans Radio Flyer. Paul died in 1995 of complications from AIDS, but I will always have our Radio Flyer memories.

Christmas Morning 1996

PAUL AND CONNIE SNEED
SCHAUMBURG, ILLINOIS

When our one-year-old son, Jeremy, woke up, my husband and I got him out of bed and brought him downstairs to the tree to see all of his gifts. There were many presents under the tree, including his Radio Flyer wagon. I ran to get my camera, to catch some memories. When I returned, Jeremy was standing in his new wagon trying to reach a candy cane. Well, I gave in, gave him the candy, and he sat in his wagon, sharing the cane with his dog. Thank you for making such a lasting toy, and memory.

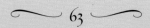

❖ Third Place ❖

CAROL A. KISTLER
MARSHALL, MISSOURI

❖ THIRD PLACE ❖

ROBYN AND BLAKE EPPS
ROLAND, ARKANSAS

Conner Epps, two weeks old, in a miniature Radio Flyer received as a baby gift. March 1997.

❖ THIRD PLACE ❖

JUDY SALISBURY
RAWSON, OHIO

The Radio Flyer wagon has always been very important to our family and brings back wonderful memories. One day my father gave my mother money to pay the property taxes at the county seat. On the way, my mother spotted a bright red Radio Flyer wagon in the window of a store and couldn't resist going in to buy it for her children. I'm sure it was quite a shock to my dad when he came home from work that evening to find a new wagon and the tax money spent. I don't remember how he scraped by that year with the taxes, but I know we spent many happy hours playing with our wagon.

Now, over fifty years later, my husband and I have our first grandson. His first Christmas present from his grandparents was a red Radio Flyer wagon. It will be a few months before he'll be big enough to sit up in the wagon, but by spring we will have a great time going up and down the driveway!

❖ Third Place ❖

Thomas D. Anderson
Manchester, Connecticut

That's me, Tommy, on the left with Spotty and my brother Jimmy. Uncle Wally bought us the Radio Flyer in 1947 when our baby brother was born. It served as our race car, our entry in the Fourth of July parade—wrapped in red, white, and blue bunting—and, covered with a cardboard box, our Conestoga wagon, until Spotty just sat down and refused his part as the young pioneers' draft horse. Our Radio Flyer lasted a long time. Its uses changed from race car to utility hauler as we grew. Now my toddler owns one, a gift for all ages.

❖ Third Place ❖

Pat Spillane
Northville, Michigan

My family lived on the crest of a hill in the Marquette Heights subdivision outside of Creve Coeur, Illinois, while I was growing up. On Christmas day when I was seven years old, I came downstairs to find a Radio Flyer wagon with my name on it in front of the tree. I was thrilled!

All winter long I loaded that wagon with toys and pulled it around the house; bumping into chairs, end tables, and other pieces of furniture. When spring came I took it outside at last and loaded it up with toys. Now, however, I'd occasionally add my dog to give her a "tour."

As the weather warmed and summer came, my father took me to get a new pair of tennis shoes, my first pair of P. F. Flyers, as I recall. Those navy shoes with the big rubber-capped toes looked really cool, and I was convinced they made me able to fly. I went home, jumped in my wagon, and, for the first time, decided to ride my wagon down that steep

hill in front of our house. I sat with one leg in the wagon and the other dangling over the side, to push off with and as a means to slow down. The first ride confirmed my belief, as I indeed did fly down the hill! It was such a great time and I mastered it so totally I rode down that hill countless times—imagine my surprise to see the big rubber-capped toes of my new shoes worn right down to the inner canvas material! My parents were even more surprised than I was . . . I wore those dilapidated shoes for about another week, as a reminder of what carelessness can cost, before they were replaced.

The Radio Flyer wagon has enabled my three children to "fly" throughout their youth and is in our children's playhouse waiting to entertain their kids. Please keep making such a quality product that helps kids learn to dream . . . and fly!

❖ Third Place ❖

**Linda Mounts
Springfield, Ohio**

Pictured in their Radio Flyer are three sisters, Barbara (eleven), Kay (five), and Linda (three) McIntire (now ages sixty-eight, sixty-two, and sixty). We had a large sloping front yard and our wagon, loaded with girls, took many trips down that hill. Linda was glad when Barbara and Kay outgrew this wagon, so she had it all to herself. It became the "family car" for her dolls and a boat on the "garage lake" when the weather prohibited outside play. Linda's son received the wooden-stake Radio Flyer at age six. He is now thirty-eight, and his three children still play with the wagon.

❖ THIRD PLACE ❖

ANTHONY DEANGELIS, III

I love my Radio Flyer to go trick-or-treating and taking walks with Mom and Dad!

❖ THIRD PLACE ❖

VICKI PORTER
FORT MILL, SOUTH CAROLINA

The year was 1951, my first birthday. My uncle gave me a red Radio Flyer—what a great present! I had room for myself, my cousin, and my doll to ride. My older cousins got to pull us. It was lots of fun.

As I grew I remember the wagon helping us carry a bucket of water from the spring, across the field, and to the house or taking it on a trip to the corner store for a bag of groceries.

Having a Radio Flyer was like having a good friend who grew up with me. Thank you for the memory.

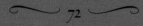

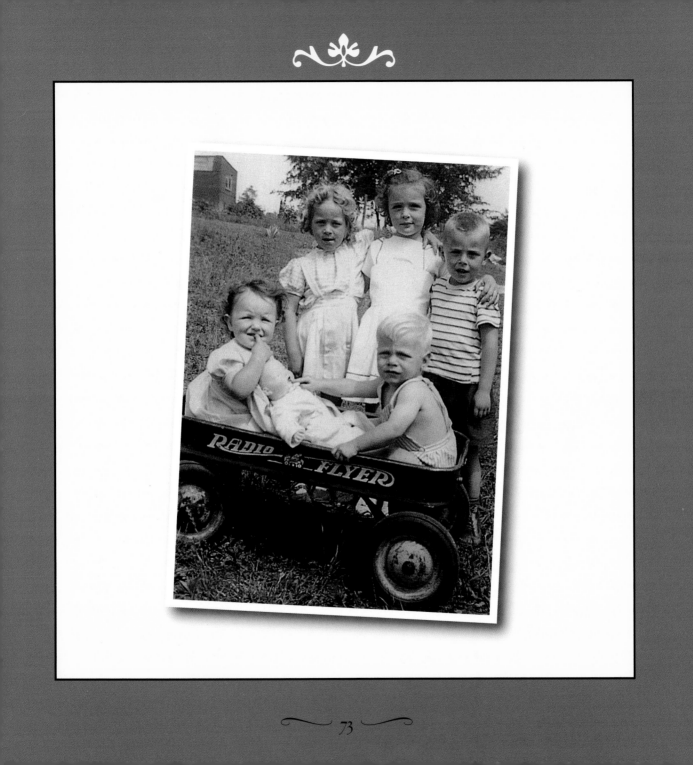

❖ THIRD PLACE ❖

KATHLEEN M. WELLS
OMAHA, NEBRASKA

I am submitting a photo for the Radio Flyer wagon contest. It was taken on Christmas Day 1951. I think you would agree those smiles tell the whole story. We still have and use our Radio Flyer wagon. It is in wonderful shape and has been used for a variety of purposes since 1951. All of the toys in the picture have long disappeared; the wagon is the only thing I have left. With the exception of the cowboy boots (long outgrown and discarded) the Radio Flyer has been the best present of that Christmas in 1951.

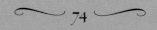

Finalists

❖ FINALISTS ❖

ELISA A. ROELS
CARY, NORTH CAROLINA

Our Radio Flyer wagon is our most precious purchase. My family uses it for walks, photo shoots at school, at the beach, at the mall, carrying dolls and toys, and most of all—for playtime. I now keep it in my van for carting the kids in and out of school with all of their belongings. We couldn't live without it. Thank you so much for making life more simple for a mother of four!

Bianca and Madison Roels

Grandma's Radio Flyer

PATRICIA J. LAMPARIELLO
PINELLAS PARK, FLORIDA

During 1953, while my husband served in the U.S. Army, I clerked at our neighborhood grocery. The storekeeper allowed me to bring my youngster with me, and my mother picked him up at noon. Little Kevin loved his daily ride in Grandma's Radio Flyer, but on the way home one day, she heard some pitiful whimpering behind her. She looked back to find her precious grandson on the sidewalk—he had tumbled out when the wheel hit a crack! Grandma lovingly cuddled him, but he wasn't pacified until she placed him back in the wagon to ride some more!

This photo of little Kevin was taken the year of the "tumble." He is now forty-five, and through the years he really got a kick out of the tale about his ride with Grandma.

SYBLE BEARD/SHAQUANSHIA JOHNSON
TULSA, OKLAHOMA

FRAN JANDA HAYNES
HAWAIIAN GARDENS, CALIFORNIA

I have memories and pictures of the Radio Flyer red wagon. I'm seventy-nine years old and I remember the uses and fun in the red wagon.

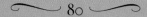

MARTHA I. DIXON
BIRMINGHAM, ALABAMA

At the time of my adoption my brother was told that my parents were getting him a little sister. When I arrived he took hold of my hand and I was indeed his. Since he was four and I was only eighteen months I couldn't ride on his tricycle. He hooked up the red wagon and rode me up and down the street. Then he would unhook the wagon and pull me up a small hill where together we could ride down. His continued imagination with that wagon has given me happy and loving memories of my childhood.

ANN HOOKS
MILLER, GEORGIA

On each of my four children and three grandchildren's second birthdays, my present to them was a shiny Radio Flyer wagon. There are lots of memories, but the most prevalent is one concerning the Radio Flyer I gave my oldest son's godson on his second birthday. When Jesse was almost three, his mother put him down for a nap and then lay down to rest. She went to sleep; he did not. He managed to unlock the door and decided to go looking for his daddy, who was at work. They lived in the country and it was almost two miles down an unpaved road to the next house. Jesse took two things with him on his excursion: his dog and his Radio Flyer wagon! He made it to the neighbor's house, and we are blessed he came to no harm. This was several years ago, but whenever I see the words "Radio Flyer wagon" I think of little Jesse walking down that road pulling his wagon.

MIKE REID
FREDERICK, MARYLAND

We purchased our Radio Flyer for our daughter, so we could walk around the block with the dog. But after seeing how much our daughter enjoyed her wagon and would sit in it waiting to go out, we started thinking back to our own childhood. My wife remembers being pulled up the street to visit her grandmother. Like most boys, I raced my wagon through the neighborhood. Our little red wagons were a big part of our youth. Thanks to Radio Flyer, our daughter will have fond memories of her childhood as well.

❖ FINALISTS ❖

EVELIA KAYLINA CARDENAS
PALM BAY, FLORIDA

My mom and dad bought me my first Radio Flyer red wagon on my first birthday. They said my eyes sparkled and I grinned from ear to ear. I liked it so much I wanted to share it with all of my bunnies, teddy bears, and dolls. We went for a drive around the neighborhood. Mom and Dad bought me my own license plate and they took pictures of my "first wheels." Thank you for making such a fun, quality product.

P.S. The box is fun too—it makes a good playhouse!

MARGARET BRICE HINES
OPP, ALABAMA

Everyone wanted to pull the bright red Radio Flyer! This humorous picture has always been a family favorite. In the eighth grade I painted a large portrait of the scene, which hangs over my bed today. The memory has always been a lighthearted way of reminding me to temper my strong-willed personality. My husband and I laugh when we look at the picture and see how much our son Robert, who is almost three years old, is like me! He, of course, has his own Radio Flyer just like the one pictured. The fun and memory making continues!

Margaret Brice Hines and Christian Elmore, Charlotte, North Carolina, summer 1970.

Red Wagon Days

MICHELE MCDONALD
OMAHA, NEBRASKA

Though the memories of my wagon are clear, memories of the person who gave it to me aren't. It was a gift from my grandpa, who died shortly after I was born. On those scorching summer days, my brother and I would pull out our wagon, then drag out the hose.

When the water was just right, we'd race over to be the first one in. Being first was best because water plunged over the sides onto the ground. Our wagon was not only fun, but part of Grandpa was there, playing with us.

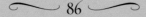

❖ FINALISTS ❖

ELKE S. DUPREE
ALPHARETTA, GEORGIA

The day our triplets, Nicholas, Annika, and Tyler, experienced their first wagon ride they had so much fun they were smiling just sitting in it! This is the only picture we have of them where all three are smiling at the same time!

The Conestoga

JEAN CANUPP
SPANISH FORT, ALABAMA

While we were growing up in the 1950s, Saturday afternoons were spent watching our favorite cowboy stars riding the range in B Westerns. So, when we found a big barrel in Grandpa's garage, it wasn't a surprise when we placed it upon our Radio Flyer and made a covered wagon. With a few acquisitions from Mother—pots and pans to hang from the sides, a jug to fill with water, bedding borrowed from my bed, and peanut butter and jelly sandwiches in a brown paper bag—we went out on a three-day journey around tiny Storden, Minnesota!

RACHEL ASHWORTH
OREM, UTAH

It was the custom on Christmas morning that we eight children had to be fully dressed, with breakfast eaten, before seeing what Santa brought. Christmas of 1940 was different. Very early, we were all awakened by the joyful voice of our four-year-old brother, who had broken the rules and sneaked to look under the tree. He ran through the house calling, "He brought me a wagon, he brought me a wagon!" in a delightful voice that only a child can make when happily surprised at Christmas. The Radio Flyer became very used and filled us all with beloved memories.

❖ FINALISTS ❖

KURT ECHOLS
CHUGIAK, ALASKA

When I went out Christmas shopping with my seventeen-month-old daughter this year, I didn't plan on purchasing a Radio Flyer red wagon for her. We were in the Costco store in Anchorage, Alaska, not far from our home, and I was trying to pick out gifts for relatives. My daughter got tired of riding in the cart and wanted to get out and walk around. She followed me through the store pretty well until we came around a corner and saw the big Radio Flyer wagon! Her eyes lit up and she ran down the aisle and tried to climb in. I helped her up and pulled her around a little bit, then she wanted to get out and pull it around herself. My mind drifted back to when I was a little boy and had a Radio Flyer wagon myself, and I remembered some very fine times pulling my toys around the backyard, racing down hills and playing with friends — all in my little red wagon. By now we were blocking the other shoppers and I tried to get her back into the cart, and she put up such a fight that I

grabbed one of the boxes off the stack and put it in the bottom of my cart, knowing how excited she would be on Christmas morning to see it under the tree.

When we opened our gifts, my mother had made me a "precious memories" scrapbook, and I smiled when I flipped to this photo, taken around 1958, of my brother and me in my old Radio Rancher wagon! Did I mention we ate lunch in our wagon too?

JOSEPHINE GIANNINI
HAMMONTON, NEW JERSEY

I am fifty-nine years old. One Christmas about ten years ago my grown son took my request for a new Radio Flyer wagon seriously and gave me one. It was an old dream come true. As a girl I wished for one. I wanted to give it to my mom. She used an old wagon for her heavy chores around the egg farm and I wanted to make it easier for her.

I use it mostly for the grandchildren. But, to this day, when I see one I can see my mom pulling that old wagon and I'm glad she had it.

❖ FINALISTS ❖

VICTORIA PONTARO
MONTEVALLO, ALABAMA

The best memory I have of Radio Flyer wagons is how much of a difference ours has made in our daughter's life. She has osteogenesis imperfecta (fragile bones) and has broken her legs five times. They put her in a body cast for a month at a time. The wagon made a lot of things possible, and life easier because she couldn't fit into a stroller. We took it everywhere we went for four months. It was suggested at Children's Hospital and has proven to be one of the best purchases we made. Now that she is walking again, she enjoys pulling it around herself and pretending her babies are hurt. Thanks for the memories, and making such quality wagons.

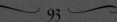

THOMAS R. ELLIOT
COTATI, CALIFORNIA

While assembling a Radio Flyer wagon for my grandson, I fondly recalled a time when God used a Radio Flyer to answer a little boy's prayer. I lived in a boarding home where the words *love* and *care* didn't exist. Every night I prayed that God would let me live with my mother again. One Christmas my friend Andy received a Radio Flyer that became our constant companion and the answer to my prayer. During one wild downhill ride, I fell out of the wagon. The next Saturday, my knee badly infected, I left that unhappy place never to return.

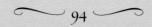

KAREN M. DEVOY
MINNEAPOLIS, MINNESOTA

My daughter heard of your contest and suggested I submit this photo of my brother and myself taken in 1947.

SHELLY BJORK
CAMBRIDGE, MINNESOTA

Our Radio Flyer had its beginnings over fifty years ago in rural Minnesota, where it was a generous supplier of many adventures for my mother on her parents' dairy farm. Over the years we have used it to haul kittens, Newfoundland puppies, each other, four babies, and even a lamb.

My favorite Radio Flyer memory is one I relive every spring when I pull it out of the garage, wheel it to our front lawn, and plant it full of flowers for the summer months while it waits for more adventures with future generations.

❖ Finalists ❖

Cynthia Vrabel
Stratford, Connecticut

Marci Gutierrez
Berkeley, Illinois

❖ FINALISTS ❖

STEVE AND JALAINE WARD
MACON, GEORGIA

Tyler Steven (three years) and Jonathon Lewis (sixteen months).

MARKO IVANEICH
FRANKFORT, ILLINOIS

Fun in the Sun with My Streak-O-Lite

MARILYN BRECHT
BLUFFTON, OHIO

Cousin Dorothy Wilch in wagon pulled by Marilyn Marquart Brecht. Received Christmas 1938.

❖ Finalists ❖

Darryl Danford
Jacksonville, Florida

Jacquelyn Marie Sletten
Albert Lea, Minnesota

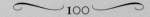

AUDREY POST
HENDERSON, KENTUCKY

Victoria's blue eyes sparkled as we picked her up from the little red wagon and held her close. She'd been diagnosed with a malignant tumor that prompted surgery to remove her left eye.

After surgery she became restless and began to whine, "I wanna ride the wagon!" How precious—after all she had been through, she just wanted to *ride the wagon*. To a two-year-old, it was a treat to be pulled in the wagon; to us, it was a memory to be cherished. The Radio Flyer helped us all *pull* through on the road to her recovery.

Janine Zambo
Columbia, Ohio

Thinking of my favorite Radio Flyer memory brought a smile to my face. When we went for walks, I put my dog, Amanda, and my little boy, Tyler, in the wagon together. They were so cute together. We got a lot of funny looks and comments from people we passed. Our dog is gone now, but we still enjoy our wagon. Next year, Tyler can share it with his baby sister, Julia.

❖ Finalists ❖

Judy Smith
Lubbock, Texas

Lucas takes a ride in his new Radio Flyer accompanied by his dogs, Christmas 1995.

❖ FINALISTS ❖

NORMAN LAVIN, M.D.
ENCINO, CALIFORNIA

1944—World War II was coming to a close, but money was still not available for anything other than basic necessities. "A Radio Flyer is out of the question!" my father screamed as tears rolled down my cheeks.

How could a five-year-old boy live without a Radio Flyer? Daily, I would walk by Jimmy's Toy Store and gaze tearfully at that beautiful red wagon sitting in the window with the price tag of $15.50 hanging from the rear wheel. But Dad said no—we can't afford it. I really understood. In the early years of the war, we hardly had enough food to eat—so a wagon was unnecessary.

But I had a plan. I asked Mr. Jimmy at the toy store if I could pay him two pennies a week (my allowance) until the bill was paid. (Did I invent the first charge account?) Believe it or not, he actually said yes. He gave me the Radio Flyer and I agreed to pay him two cents a week until the $15.50 was paid in full. I guess he didn't know about interest in those days.

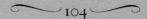

As my allowance increased, I increased my weekly payment. I never missed a week and I never missed the candy I would have bought had I kept my allowance. But instead I had the most beautiful Radio Flyer in the world.

1998 — Fifty-four years later, my son is almost five years old, and he's asked me to buy him a Radio Flyer that he saw at our local department store. He must have it, he tells me, and we *can* afford it, he adds. "Maybe so," I reply, "but it will cost you two cents a week from your allowance until you are all paid up." "Are you kidding Dad?" "No son," I say. "Let me tell you a story that took place long before you were born. The year was 1944 . . . "

MARGE HICKEY
OMAHA, NEBRASKA

Would you like a ride?" Dad asked as he opened the car door. We loaded our little red wagon and Mason jar full of water into the back seat and silently rode home. No one questioned us. Had Mom called Dad home from the office to look for us? Did he just happen to be driving this way and just happened to see us, outside of town, three miles from home? Seventy years later, we still wonder why those two little girls were walking so far away from their happy home.

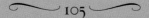

Sergei P. Naramore
Whitney Point, New York

I was too young to remember getting my first Radio Flyer as a present from Grandma, but I do remember my Radio Flyer always being there as one of the mainstays while growing up.

After my father died in July of 1947, my mother, sister, and I lived upstairs in a two-family house in Marathon, New York. As we had no car, my Radio Flyer made many trips with us to the store. I only had a few toys, but I had my Radio Flyer and I could pedal it anywhere and everywhere, and I did.

I have countless memories of me and my Radio Flyer, but my favorite is one of the most recent. I am fifty-four now and still have a Radio Flyer, albeit a newer one (a Model 95 made for True Value Hardware), which I introduced to my grandson last Labor Day weekend. My daughter and I pulled him around while taking a rare walk together (they live in Wisconsin). Upon returning home I went in the house to get the camera. As I came back out I looked to see the two of them whizzing down the road in our park laughing at the top of their lungs. I ran over just in time to hear my grandson exclaim, "Mom, next time from the top!"

The fun and joy of a Radio Flyer truly roll through the generations!

In these photos I was just over four years old. Already there are many scrapes and scratches on my well-used Radio Flyer, as well as a missing hubcap from my playing mechanic.

The pose of my right knee in the wagon and left leg pedaling show the way I "drove" my Radio Flyer everywhere I went.

❖ FINALISTS ❖

TIMOTHY CRAIG
SHUSHAN, NEW YORK

Pittsburgh is a blue-collar San Francisco with its many steep hills, and it was down one of these, Elm Street, that I was coasting in my Radio Flyer on a fall day in 1949. Before my eyes, marooned at the center of the intersection of Elm and the brilliantly named Hill Avenue, was a small girl, no more than three years old. Approaching her was a driverless Studebaker, whose driver had failed to park her with the wheels turned to the curb. I instantly shifted to one knee in my wagon, accelerating as never before with the other foot, and collected the tot a moment before the runaway vehicle swept over the spot she had occupied. Her father, it turned out, was the mystically respected coach of our high school football team, Clark T. Miller, and a few years later he included me in his lineup as a free safety in a locale where football has religious overtones.

Clark T. Miller, not to mention Studebaker, has left the stage, but Radio Flyer, I'm happy to learn, has not.

❖ FINALISTS ❖

SHIRLEY J. PATTERSON
CLARKSBURG, WEST VIRGINIA

The year was 1960 when we purchased our Radio Flyer wagon. It was a Christmas present for our two-month-old son, Mark. He spent Christmas Day asleep in his new wagon. We have kept the wagon all these years. Mark is now thirty-seven years old and has a three-year-old daughter.

The Radio Flyer wagon is still in great shape. Nancy Jo Patterson enjoys using the wagon to haul her teddy bears and dolls around, and also likes her grandpa to pull her around the yard.

Nancy should enjoy her Radio Flyer wagon for many years and someday pass it on to her own children.

MARILYN PRITCHARD
ELM GROVE, WISCONSIN

The Radio Flyer pictured here was enjoyed by my three older sisters and me for many childhood years before retiring to my mother's garage. One year, she pulled it out, dusted it off, and had it fully restored, including having the logo repainted. She presented it to my young nephew, Robbie, as a Christmas present that year. Needless to say, he was over-joyed to find it under the Christmas tree, but after all the excitement of opening gifts, he climbed in and promptly fell asleep!

❖ FINALISTS ❖

JOSEPH ANDERSON
DIX HILLS, NEW YORK

I was only three days old when I received my red Radio Flyer wagon. My Aunt Laura and Uncle Richie brought it for me. It was filled with baby clothes and wrapped in cellophane paper. After looking at all the clothes, my mother insisted I *try the wagon on*. After all, I only weighed five pounds and three ounces, and would be too big soon enough. It was a perfect fit!

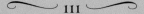

❖ FINALISTS ❖

WILLIAM CLOSE
CEDAR FALLS, IOWA

Each year the students at Peet Junior High School in Cedar Falls, Iowa, construct a monumental outdoor mega-sculpture. This year the students elected to build a giant wagon. While planning the sculpture the students were polled to determine their favorite memory with their wagons. A majority of students recalled filling their wagons with toys or pets and having a parade. The resulting sculpture was a Radio Flyer wagon with a Beanie Baby puppy aboard. The students at Peet Junior High had a wonderful experience building this sculpture and would love to know what you think of their wagon.

How My Radio Flyer and I Helped Win World War II

STEPHEN PRESS
POUGHQUAG, NEW YORK

On December 7, 1941, America went to war, and the children of America were asked to help. Scrap was needed. Old tires could become new tires for a Jeep. Waste paper could become boxes for medicine. A clothes iron could become a helmet. One junk radiator could make a bomb. Along with thousands of other boys and girls I went from house to house, and loaded my Radio Flyer wagon with the tools our fighting men and women needed. We weren't old enough to fight, but we could do our part. We couldn't have done it without our sturdy Radio Flyer wagons.

❖ FINALISTS ❖

BETTY WILSON
PITTSBORO, NORTH CAROLINA

Picnic Wagon!

❖ FINALISTS ❖

TED AND HELEN GREEN
SPOKANE, WASHINGTON

This is a picture of our daughter, Susan, and her brother Bob. She received this Radio Flyer wagon for her first birthday, June 4, 1946. We kept it at home until she married, then later her two boys enjoyed it and really gave it a good workout. Below is a picture of Susan with her wagon now. Her brother Bob repainted it a while back, and her husband made her a planter box for it.

Our whole family has wonderful memories, with snapshots and 8mm movies of the Radio Flyer wagon.

❖ FINALISTS ❖

DIANA ANDERSON
SPOKANE, WASHINGTON

This photo is special to many people because all three boys are three years old in the picture and, most importantly, all three are adopted children. On this day they were celebrating Jordan's birthday. He had just gotten the wagon from his parents. Alex (far right) got a wagon for Christmas, just like his best buddy Jordan's!

❖ FINALISTS ❖

THELMA D. WILTSHIRE
SACRAMENTO, CALIFORNIA

Since 1934, I have owned six red wagons and have given Radio Flyers to three of my great-grandchildren. During World War II, when gasoline was scarce, I tied my red wagon to my bicycle to go to the store and take my children to my mother's house and the park. My tandem vehicle became the most reliable means of transportation and has become a lifelong memory. In 1970, my dad bought me another red wagon, which I still have today. In 1995, I bought my first Radio Flyer for my great-grandchildren's enjoyment.

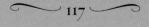

MRS. L. H. MICKELSON
FRESNO, CALIFORNIA

July 1949 found three-year-old William Michael Mickelson in Adrian, Michigan, with a red Radio Flyer wagon and his black cat, Satan. They both enjoyed rides whenever Grandpa, Grandma, or Mama pulled them around the yard. At least Mike enjoyed it— Satan mostly endured it and then decided to bail out. That left Mike alone and smiling hopefully that *someone* would come along and make it go.

❖ FINALISTS ❖

COLLEEN LIGGETT
CORAOPOLIS, PENNSYLVANIA

Here is a picture of my son, Alex, and my husband, Matthew. Our favorite memory of our Radio Flyer is going on walks together. As soon as we would get up the hill, Alex would be fast asleep. He's on the verge of falling asleep in the picture!

A Few of My Favorite Things . . .

ABBEY CATHERINE ROBINSON
BEAUFORT, SOUTH CAROLINA

My favorite afternoon event is riding my Radio Flyer Town and Country wagon to feed the horsey who lives down the street. One day, my best friend Katie and I dressed up in our favorite hats, loaded my wagon with apples for the horsey and dog biscuits for the barn puppies and snacks for ourselves. Mommy pulled us down the street for a picnic with our animal friends.

❖ Finalists ❖

Linda McAnally
Booneville, Arkansas

KARYN THOMAS
OOLOGAH, OKLAHOMA

In 1963 my sister Debbie and I were eight and nine. We lived in California in a row of new brick houses. We loved to pull the little red wagon up the alley looking for pop bottles. Each small bottle was worth a nickel, and if we were lucky enough to get a large one, it might bring a dime. One of us might pull the other; as we scoured our neighbors' trash for treasures, the wagon would run out of room, and we would finally return home with enough income for candy bars, soda pops, or Popsicles!

Only Empty Wagons Make Noise

NORMAN P. DeTULLIO
TRUMBULL, CONNECTICUT

Only empty wagons make noise. But mine was, after all, a Radio Flyer, and it sang a special song as it whooshed me through a childhood full of promises. With Muggs by my side we churned down Sentinel Hill, riding the gravitational pull of the moon and the stars.

When I turned twelve my Radio Flyer winked into view for one last time from beneath a mountain of melting snow. That summer, with Muggs still by my side, I took my last ride.

Now, forty years later, it rests amid rafters, a silent reminder of that grand race out of childhood, a handle length away from the promises it kept.

❖ FINALISTS ❖

ROBERT A. SHELLADY
IOWA CITY, IOWA

Radio Flyer. Magic words to the smiling six-year-old showing off his new baby brother in August 1942, in a cherished "coaster wagon." I was sure there was a connection to radio heroes Jack Armstrong, Sergeant Preston, and Captain Midnight that propelled my soaring imagination. "Flyer" was sure proof of that, linked to the P-38s and B-17s that fascinated and reassured me that the darkening clouds of World War II, begun just months ago, would be parted in shining victory. I flew many an exciting "mission" in my Radio Flyer!

With the war safely behind us in June 1948, the Radio Flyer became a part of our imaginary journey to the Old West of Gene Autrey and Roy Rogers as a cozy covered wagon in my thirteen-year-old mind.

Now that I'm a sixty-year-old grandfather, these "little red wagon memories" came rolling back as I purchased a shiny new Town and Country wagon for my beautiful granddaughter and another for a grandson just born. I can hope their Radio Flyers will be so filled with pleasant memories. But, after all, that part is "assembly required" on their part!

❖ FINALISTS ❖

SUSAN PELINSKI
PARK RIDGE, ILLINOIS

Long before McDonald's Happy Meals I had my Happy Wheels—
my Radio Flyer little red wagon.
Except it only looked like a wagon
to others—to me it was . . .
A race car! I was the first woman race-car
driver in the Indy 500—of course
I won!
A rocket ship to the moon, speeding at a
jillion miles an hour!
A yellow bus to carry my doll-children
to school! Now, my flying days
are over, but this Christmas, my
grandchildren will get the "gift
of wings"—their own Radio
Flyer little red wagon.

RON CRUGER
HONOLULU, HAWAII

It was 1936 in the Bronx. All that mattered to me was that the Yankees won the pennant and then the World Series. I was four years old and the doctors had diagnosed me with rheumatic fever. The treatment was for me to lie in bed until my condition improved. My only contact with the world outside my bedroom was each afternoon when my father came home from work. He lined the bed of my Radio Flyer with a blanket and a pillow and placed me in the center of the wagon and took me for a forty-five-minute journey around the neighborhood. I sat quietly in the Radio Flyer and Dad dutifully pulled me around the neighborhood. Dad waved at neighbors, introducing me to everyone he knew, and even those he did not. Every day of my young life I waited for my dad to get off work and come home to lift me into the Flyer and pull me around the streets. For four years all I knew of the outside world I discovered from my position inside my Radio Flyer. Dad is gone, as is my wagon, but my memories of both have filled my heart for over half a century.

❖ FINALISTS ❖

JOSEPH L. TERAMAW
HUDSON, OHIO

My Radio Flyer provided more than just fun rides as I was growing up. Both Mom and Dad died when I was eight, leaving three boys and three girls alone, with the oldest being sixteen—she took care of us! My Radio Flyer was used to collect bottles for the return money. Those bottles were what was left of weekly fraternity parties at a nearby college. The extra money meant we could have milk instead of water on our breakfast cereal! I am now sixty-eight years old and happy to have a chance to say "Thanks, Radio Flyer," for being there!

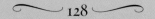

❖ FINALISTS ❖

KATHERINE HAYES
SAINT MARTINVILLE, LOUISIANA

I'll never forget my Radio Flyer red wagon. I got mine when I was twenty-three. My husband and I married very young. At twenty-three I had four kids. We didn't own an automobile, so visiting was limited. We lived way out in the country. Our closest neighbor lived about a city block away. Yet with so many small children, even visiting my neighbors was out of the question. The Christmas of 1971 my husband gave me my Radio Flyer wagon. I would load the kids in that wagon every afternoon and was finally able to visit my friends and neighbors.

❖ Finalists ❖

Pam Hansen
Hopewell Junction, New York

I have many wonderful memories of time spent on my Radio Flyer as a kid. It seems to me that life as a child in the sixties was spent more creatively, thinking of new ways to entertain ourselves. My sister and I spent many days and drove many miles into worlds unknown in our Radio Flyer. The most outstanding memory was the day we decided we didn't want to clean our room anymore. Our parents were being unfair and expected too much. We decided the time had come to set out on our own. We packed our precious belongings and even included half a package of saltines and a mayonnaise jar full of water, surely enough to survive long enough to teach our parents a lesson. Well, soon the crackers and water ran out and we started bickering over whose turn it was to pull the wagon. We decided it was time to go back home. A full half-hour had passed, plenty of time for our parents to regret treating us so horribly.

That story took place about thirty-five years ago, and I was recently reminded of it when my own children decided that life was unfair, their parents expected too much, and that they wanted to teach us a lesson.

They all packed up their belongings and food for the journey and said a very somber good-bye. Theirs was not an easy route, however, since they had to pull their Radio Flyer through two feet of snow. As my husband and I stood waving at the window, trying to show emotion and concern, I felt history repeat itself. One by one the kids came home, one because he was hungry, one because he was cold, and finally our daughter returned, furious her brothers had deserted her.

I look forward to the day that my grandchildren board their Radio Flyer and head for the hills. It is truly an experience we all must face, a great lesson for all generations.

❖ FINALISTS ❖

CAROL M. EDENS
SAINT PETE BEACH, FLORIDA

In 1985, Hurricane Elaina hit Tampa, Florida. My husband, Earl, was a patient at Tampa General Hospital, and the decision to evacuate was made. I was there, caring for my husband, preparing him for an airlift to another hospital. I went to the lobby to help and witnessed hundreds of young people assisting people to awaiting buses, ten-wheelers, ambulances, and vans. Then a parade of red Radio Flyer wagons appeared, pulling infants and many young patients from the pediatric wards. The expected cries were few—most seemed to enjoy the ride!

❖ FINALISTS ❖

SHEILA BRIGHT
OAK GROVE, MISSOURI

It was hard times in the 1950s for my mom, raising two children on her own. During harvest and planting seasons we walked to her uncle's farm to work in the fields. More often than not, it was well after dark when we headed home, my brother and I tucked securely in our Radio Flyer on a soft quilt, sharing space with fruits and vegetables sent with us for our labors. We often fell asleep, lulled by Mom's gentle voice singing softly down the country road toward home.

❖ FINALISTS ❖

VALERIE DIDRIKSON
LOMBARD, ILLINOIS

My brother Gary didn't want Mom stopping the wagon (as you can probably tell from his expression)—not even for a picture! He just wanted to get going. He still talks fondly of his favorite red wagon!
—Gary Joseph Olsen, 1951

❖ FINALISTS ❖

LAURIE DICKIE
MIDLAND, TEXAS

My favorite memory of the Radio Flyer is the photo I had taken of my nine-month-old son, Dalton, sitting on his wagon. Before the session, I was scrambling around the house looking for an interesting prop. I took the wagon because the colors went well with my son's outfit and the Fourth of July theme. The picture turned out great— it was as though Dalton was ready to go flying in his little red Radio Flyer!

JEAN C. SANTARELLI
EGG HARBOR, NEW JERSEY

I miss my dad. These pictures were taken December 25, 1952.

❖ FINALISTS ❖

ALMA HOBBS
GOULDBUSK, TEXAS

Clayton Wilson wanted a big red wagon for his third Christmas. This was his dream. His grandparents gave him a miniature wagon a few days before Christmas. To make Christmas more magical, we placed his miniature wagon under the tree on Christmas Eve, then had him sprinkle it with "magic powder," say "Abracadabra," and off he went to bed. Santa came, and *poof!* When Clayton got up on Christmas morning, a huge wagon was there. He still believes, four years later, that at Christmas anything can happen!

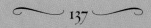

❖ FINALISTS ❖

BONNIE SUE BASTIN
NEWTON, NEW JERSEY

I treasure the memory of a little girl and a little red wagon. Shortly before her second birthday, our daughter Rebekah required major abdominal surgery. Although the operation was a success, she would not eat or drink until a visit was arranged with her brothers.

During her recovery at home, the boys noticed many children with wagons. They insisted Rabekah needed a wagon too.

The surgery is behind us now and the painful memories are fading, but I will always cherish the day three big brothers took turns, proudly pulling their little sister in her new Radio Flyer wagon.

❖ Finalists ❖

Jodi Frazier
Highlands Ranch, Colorado

TWILLA MCCARTHY
RAPID CITY, SOUTH DAKOTA

Growing up on a farm in Nebraska in the 1950s, we had few toys. We did, however, have a Radio Flyer wagon that gave us endless hours of fun. With a little imagination it could be anything we wanted, from a doll buggy to a covered wagon. There was a small hill in front of our house. My two older sisters and I spent hours riding down it in the wagon. Not only did we pull our dolls and teddy bears in it, but the kittens, puppies, and ducklings were often given rides.

Today when I picture the farmhouse where I grew up, I see the wagon sitting there in the yard under a big cottonwood tree. It brings back such beautiful memories of carefree summer days spent playing there. This year for Christmas I bought my own grandchildren Radio Flyer wagons, in the hope that they'll get as much enjoyment from theirs as we did ours.

SHARON J. EPPLER
GREENFIELD, INDIANA

I celebrated my fifth birthday in September of 1952 on my grandfather's farm in New Sharon, Maine. My grandfather had asked me to help him milk the cows; but instead of a cow in the first stall, there was a new shiny red Radio Flyer!

Over the years, my four younger sisters and I found a lot of creative uses for the wagon—a pretend car, transportation for the family cats, and more. When I had two sons of my own in the 1970s, they found even more uses for the wagon—a racing car, junk hauler, whatever! My wagon was also used for practical purposes, such as hauling rocks from our garden and wood for our fireplace.

Although my wagon isn't shiny anymore, it is still very precious to me and has gone with me from the New England states to California, and now to my new home in the Midwest.

❖ FINALISTS ❖

DIANE HARTWIG
EATON, OHIO

My first Radio Flyer experience was when I was five years old. It was the evening before Easter, when we always went to my grandparents' house (with all of the aunts, uncles, and cousins) and spent the night there. I remember feeling so excited for the Easter Bunny to come that I could hardly sleep. The next morning, much to my surprise, there was a wagon, full of candy. I squealed with delight.

Yet this cannot compare to the experience of giving a red Radio Flyer wagon to my daughter. Seeing her "squeal with delight" is even more special. Now I know how my mom must have felt on that special Easter day.

❖ FINALISTS ❖

SHARI ZYCHINSKI
FAIRWAY, KANSAS

Our Radio Flyer had enough room for my Oscar Mayer puppets, my blue blanket, a snack pack, and my little sister, Bonni. I pulled this wagonful to the edge of our backyard, which ended with a woods full of high trees. We stopped, seemingly so far away from the house, and spread the blanket out in the wagon. I put on a Magic Weenie and Friends puppet show while Bonni watched, munching string cheese and saltines in the corner of the wagon. Then we both ate the cookies and shared the Cinderella thermos full of milk.

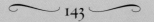